Original title:
The Answer to Life's Meaning? Still Pending

Copyright © 2025 Creative Arts Management OÜ
All rights reserved.

Author: Harris Montgomery
ISBN HARDBACK: 978-1-80566-224-2
ISBN PAPERBACK: 978-1-80566-519-9

Time's Silent Inquiry

Tick-tock goes the clock, so loud,
But answers hide beneath the cloud.
We chase our tails in circles round,
While wisdom giggles, lost then found.

A fish once sighed in ocean deep,
As questions swirled in bubbles, leap.
Each riddle wrapped in jests and glee,
Ah, the joy of not knowing, carefree!

Threads of Uncertainty

In the tapestry of time, we weave,
Threads so tangled, who to believe?
A cat in a hat nods with a grin,
As we ponder if this is where we begin.

A donut's hole holds secrets tight,
Is it a point or a missing bite?
The more we laugh, the less we find,
Perhaps we're meant to be left behind!

The Incomplete Puzzle

A puzzle box with pieces few,
Trying to fit the odd with new.
Corners never seem to align,
But hey, at least we have some wine!

Once I met a sock at a bar,
He claimed he'd traveled quite far.
Together we laughed as pieces flew,
This jigsaw life, a whimsical zoo!

A Journey Through Infinite Roads

With maps that fold and twist away,
We journey through the light of day.
A sign that says 'this way, not that',
As squirrels debate where they sat.

A penguin slides down icy trails,
While questioning the why in tales.
We roam the paths with simple cheer,
Wondering what's hiding over here!

Unwritten Chapters of Tomorrow

Pages blank, with scribbles near,
A pen in hand, but filled with fear.
Tomorrow's tales still not unfurled,
Guessing plots in a crazy world.

The sun will rise with tales untold,
Or maybe just some soup that's cold.
We write and laugh, to dodge despair,
A comedy of thoughts laid bare.

Unanswered Questions at Dusk

Why do socks disappear so quick?
Do they escape on some secret trip?
The clock strikes questions, loud mistake,
As laughter dances, shadows wake.

Are stars just holes in someone's jeans?
Is life a sitcom with unseen scenes?
At dusk we ponder, wine in hand,
All the answers slip like sand.

The Quest for Clarity

Set out with snacks, and drinks in tow,
Searching for wisdom, or a tasty pro.
In maps of thought, we twist and turn,
With every step, we live and learn.

A treasure hunt for inner peace,
Or just a quest for some grilled cheese?
Each clue we find, confuses us more,
Each bite we take, we just adore.

Mirages of Understanding

Like a desert's dance, mirage we chase,
Thoughts appear, then lose their place.
Are we alone or part of the scheme?
Life's just a multi-colored dream.

With compasses that spin around,
We map the nonsense, lost then found.
Laughter echoes, wisdom's thin,
In this circus, where to begin?

Gentle Ripples of Doubt

In a world where socks are mismatched,
I ponder if that's quite attached.
Do ducks ever think, "What's a quack?"
Or is that their way of keeping track?

The cat flies by, in a cardboard box,
While I wonder, do I make better flocks?
If my toast lands butter-side down,
Is that the universe trying to clown?

The plants in my room seem to judge me,
As I dance like no one's ever free.
Does a confused cactus ever pout,
Or is it just part of the plant route?

While ants march forth, I lose the thread,
Of cosmic questions dance in my head.
Do aliens giggle at Earthly woes?
Or simply observe as the laughter grows?

Questions Beneath the Surface

Why did the chicken cross the street?
To find a clue, not just to eat.
With questions bubbling, laughter grows,
As logic dances, no one knows.

The cat just naps, it has the time,
While fish debate in bubbles, prime.
The dog just barks at passing cars,
Wonders if life's hidden in Mars.

A pirouette of thoughts in air,
While squirrels plot with utmost flair.
With whispers shared between the trees,
And giggles triggered by the breeze.

The ducks quack loud, who's got the map?
In search of truth, they set the trap.
Yet every fact they try to find,
Just leads them back to playful mind.

Echoes of a Thousand Thoughts

In the library, books spill their tales,
Confused, they shuffle, through countless trails.
A thought once stuck, now dances bold,
Looking for answers, oh so cold.

The toaster pops, a crumb takes flight,
It lands on wisdom, feels just right.
While coffee cups chat, fueled by beans,
Debating life's quirks with frothy scenes.

The clock ticks on with a funny face,
It laughs at time, a slow-paced race.
Echoes bounce from wall to wall,
In this wacky circus, we all fall.

With paper planes and dreams so bright,
We question stars that shine at night.
Collecting whims like fading light,
In this grand jest, we laugh in flight.

The Great Unraveling

Oh look, a sock has gone astray,
It tangled up with thoughts today.
In laundry's realm, lost threads unfold,
Spinning tales that tickle the bold.

The sweater's yarn, a web of dreams,
Untwisting now, or so it seems.
Each pull reveals a story odd,
And fate's great plan seems kinda flawed.

A puzzle's corner whispers sweet,
While jigsaw pieces dodge defeat.
In this chaos, some giggles rise,
As life's a riddle in duck disguise.

Elastic bands stretch to the skies,
To catch the truths, but oh, what lies!
In the great unravel, we all play,
With laughter, hopes, and socks, hooray!

Between Dreams and Reality

Bouncing between what's real and not,
The cat believes it's won the lot.
Chasing shadows, a race so wild,
In dreamlike states, they frolic, mild.

The coffee spills, a canvas white,
Each drip a dream both bold and slight.
Sugar cubes conspire to play along,
While spoons debate what's right or wrong.

The morning fog, a cloak of fears,
Whispers secrets in hushéd cheers.
In slumber's realm, all bets are fair,
As waking life just stops to stare.

With silly hats and mismatched socks,
We dance through gates and ticking clocks.
In the in-between, where laughter reigns,
Life spirals on, despite the chains.

The Light at Dusk

The sun dips low, what a sight,
But questions linger, what feels right?
With shadows creeping, we all laugh,
Where's the manual for this craft?

The crickets chirp, the owls hoot,
Life's like a dance, not a commute.
Yet here we are, all feeling dazed,
Stuck in a puzzle, all amazed!

The Linger of Questions

Why's pizza round, packed in a square?
Why do we stop to ponder air?
Life's a circus, a comical show,
Who ties the knots of fate, do you know?

We search for wisdom in cookies, they say,
But all I get's crumbs at the end of the day.
With dreams in pockets, confusion in tow,
We ride on the carousel, round and slow.

A Symphony of Unanswered Notes

I took a swing at a mindset grand,
But fell flat, oh wasn't it planned?
With perplexed symphonies under the moon,
The bandwagon's here, but I'm out of tune.

Echoes of laughter dance in the air,
Where's the conductor? Does he even care?
In this wild rhapsody of thought and cheer,
We strum to questions, the punchlines near!

Driftwood on the Ocean of Uncertainty

Waves crash high, oh what a thrill,
Wondering if time's a massive swill.
Driftwood floats past, carrying dreams,
Our hopes like bubbles, bursting at seams.

Navigating seas of 'what if' and 'why',
While fish-eye questions swim right by.
With chuckles and grins, we sail along,
To the unknown shores, we all belong.

Navigating a Sea of Thoughts

Waves crash and splash with glee,
Sailing on thoughts that might be free.
Navigating through the quirky tides,
With a map where rhyme and reason hides.

Questions float like jellyfish,
Hoping for a wild, witty wish.
Dancing on currents of sheer delight,
Lost in the maze but feeling quite right.

Seagulls squawk with very little care,
While I ponder life from my sandy chair.
Searching for pearls in a sea of clams,
With no clue to guide me, just silly jams.

I set sail with a hefty grin,
Not caring if I'll ever win.
For in this caper of thought's gentle trip,
I'm just a sailor on a funny little ship.

Footprints in the Sand of Time

Footprints scatter on a sunlit shore,
Each one a question, maybe more.
Some lead to wisdom, some to a laugh,
Tracing the path of my own daft craft.

The tide rolls in, erasing my trace,
A comical game in this timeless race.
Like a child drawing shapes in the sand,
Hoping the tide understands my plan.

Chasing the waves with a gleeful shout,
Wondering if I'll figure it out.
Each step I take with a skip and hop,
In this sandy dance, I just can't stop!

So I laugh alongside the gulls that play,
While pondering thoughts that drift away.
What fun to wander, what fun to roam,
In a fleeting world that feels like home.

Breaths Between Questions

Inhale the queries, exhale the jest,
A funny riddle that never lets rest.
Between each breath lies a curious pause,
Wondering if I should just take a cause.

The world spins on, what a silly game,
With each second gone, who's really to blame?
Moments escape like bubbles in air,
Sparkling questions, a whimsical affair.

Caught in a whirlwind of ponder and jest,
What comes next? Oh, that's anyone's guess!
But giggles and grins keep me afloat,
Drifting through life in a silly little boat.

So here's to the questions that tickle my mind,
In each puff of laughter, I'll seek and I'll find.
For in the pauses, my joy takes flight,
In the dance of the day, everything feels right.

The Silence of Seeking

In silence I sit with a perplexed face,
Trying to solve life's wild, wacky pace.
With giggles echoing in the quiet air,
Seeking the wisdom that's hidden somewhere.

Pondering deeply while sipping on tea,
What would a fish think of being a bee?
Questions like butterflies fluttering near,
Each one tickling my mind with a cheer.

In this hush, I find a comedic spark,
Like a cat in the night that forgot how to bark.
The more that I search, the funnier it gets,
The universe chuckles, but no one forgets.

So here I shall linger, enjoying the ride,
With laughter as my very best guide.
For the search might be funny, a sight to behold,
In the silence of seeking, I'm endlessly told.

Beyond the Horizon of Knowing

There's a land where wisdom goes to nap,
A place where answers wear a silly cap.
The squirrels debate in cosmic jest,
While the owls just sleep through every quest.

A wise old turtle walks with a grin,
Saying, 'Life's a game; you can't always win.'
As we chase ideas like fleeting fireflies,
The truth ducks and hides, a master of disguise.

Cracks in the Facade of Certainty

In a world where all truths lightly dance,
Certainty's costume slips at first glance.
The philosophers trip on their own wise quotes,
As the universe giggles, and softly gloats.

The crystal ball breaks, and oh what a sight,
It reveals that confusion can actually bite.
A parrot squawks out profound yet bizarre,
'Life's just a mystery wrapped in a jar!'

Shadows of Forgotten Truths

In a cupboard of wisdom, dusty and dim,
Lie shadows of truths that once shone like whim.
The echoes of laughter, they curiously spark,
While reality whispers, 'Just don't lose the mark.'

The cat on the shelf has a tale to share,
About dilemmas that float in midair.
With each fallen thought, a new joke appears,
As laughter blends sweetly with curious fears.

The Unfolding Paradox

In a circus of thoughts twirling around,
The ringmaster chuckles without making a sound.
Life's puns and riddles, a slapstick affair,
Where whispers of wisdom hang thick in the air.

A juggling act of what's right and wrong,
As the audience hums an uncertain song.
We flip and we flop in our quest to be wise,
And truths become pranks, much to our surprise.

The Duality of Knowing

In a world of black and white,
Wisdom wears a clown's delight.
Questions hang like stars in space,
Answers lost without a trace.

What's to gain, what's to lose?
Flip a coin, it's just a ruse.
With each truth, a jest arrives,
We dance like bees with busy hives.

Knowing more, yet oh so less,
Life's a riddle, we all guess.
Laughing loud at life's big show,
Ah, the jokes we hardly know!

So here we stand, a funny crew,
Wading in what's vague yet true.
Embrace the chaos, take a spin,
In this circus, we all grin!

Keys to Locked Doors

I found a key, the size of me,
But which door locks, I cannot see.
One swings left, another right,
Which will lead to wondrous sights?

I jingle keys, they sing and chime,
Still stuck in place, it's about time.
Knocking twice, I tap my feet,
'Hello? Anyone home?' Sounds quite sweet.

Doors may be locked or just ajar,
What's behind? A book or a jar?
With open minds and giggles loud,
We'll browse the shelves, be unbowed.

So shake your keys and strike a pose,
What lies beyond? Who really knows?
We laugh and skip from door to door,
Unlocking fun, forevermore!

Shadows Cast by Illumination

A lightbulb flickers, or is it just me?
Shadows dance like they're wild and free.
Lurking corners with secret smiles,
Join the fun, stay for a while!

Shapes that stretch and twist with glee,
One looks like my grandma, can it be?
I laugh so hard, my sides do ache,
Each shadow's story, make no mistake.

Flick of a switch, and they take flight,
What stories spin in the dead of night?
In this comedy of light and dark,
Shadows play on, a lovely lark.

So let's embrace this playful game,
Chasing shadows, who's to blame?
Join the cast of whimsical jests,
In this theater, where laughter rests!

In Search of the Unbearable Lightness

We set off hoping for something grand,
But the journey's map just won't expand.
What's heavy here, what's light as air?
In the search, we find silly flair.

A feather floats, then a rock does too,
We giggle at what's stuck like glue.
Carrying burdens that weigh our hearts,
Yet laughter lifts, and that's where it starts.

We ponder deeply, yet laugh out loud,
Searching for wisdom, we feel quite proud.
With every twist and wobbly flight,
We turn our search into delight.

So here's to the quests we undertake,
With each misstep, more laughs we make.
For in our search, we find the treat,
Life's absurdities, a joyful feat!

Beyond the Horizon of Understanding

In a world where socks go missing,
We ponder while the cat is hissing.
Is it deep, or just a farce?
Maybe life's just one big sparse.

With coffee spills like tiny floods,
We muse on life through all the suds.
Is a sandwich worth the chatter?
Or is it just a plate of flatter?

When questions knock, like pesky pests,
We throw confetti, call it quests.
So many thoughts, yet none that land,
Just jokes and riddles, all unplanned.

At the brink of night we chuckle,
Nonsense wraps around our knuckle.
In the end, we might just find,
A punchline left to tease the mind.

The Silent Odyssey

Sailing ships of silly dreams,
Drifting on a sea of memes.
Navigators lost in delight,
Chasing shadows, then taking flight.

Quiet nights and rambunctious days,
Life unfolds in funny ways.
We scratch our heads and laugh a bit,
Is that a clue, or just a split?

With rubber ducks and funny hats,
We dance like strange and happy cats.
Each riddle leads to paths amiss,
But who cares? We're here for the bliss.

In libraries of laughter loud,
We write stories, feel so proud.
But amidst the joy, we just might find,
The punchline hid in life's unwind.

Fragments of a Lingering Puzzle

Puzzles scattered, pieces lost,
Finding them comes at a cost.
With every fit, we laugh and sigh,
Like trying to make a giraffe fly.

A squirrel glances with sly delight,
As we trip over thoughts, a sight!
Can we solve the great unknown?
Or just gather dust, like an old bone?

With every tick of time, we jest,
Questions rise, we never rest.
Is life a game of hide and seek?
Or just a carnival, so unique?

In corners of our scattered mind,
Fragments left, perplexed and blind.
But still we giggle, life's a show,
A comedy where none can know.

Beneath the Gray Skies of Reason

Beneath the clouds that gloom and sway,
We laugh at logic's funny play.
With jokes like rain, they softly fall,
Impossibly wise? Not at all.

In the café, mugs raised high,
We ponder truth as birds fly by.
Is wisdom just a clever ruse?
Or merely tea, with different brews?

Statistics claim we're all astray,
Yet here we are, come what may.
In the realm of quirky thought,
Sanity's something we've all bought.

So we embrace the cloudy night,
With goofy grins, our hearts take flight.
For in the chaos, laughter sings,
And that alone? A lovely thing.

Glimmers of an Elusive Truth

In a field of vibrant dreams,
A goat claims the wisdom seams.
It munches grass, snorts with glee,
Oh, to crack this mystery!

Philosophers with hats so tall,
Debate the purpose of it all.
One says, 'Pizza!'—the crowd agrees,
Thus, happiness is simply cheese.

A cat on a window sill,
Stares at the world, plotting its thrill.
It ponders life's quirks with sass,
While chasing shadows, it lets time pass.

And here we laugh, a merry crew,
For answers hide in plain view.
With jest and laughter, we shall roam,
Finding joy in the unknown home.

The Horizon's Perplexity

The sun dips low with a silly grin,
As if it knows where we've been.
Clouds whisper secrets, but they're shy,
Teasing truths while floating by.

A squirrel dances on a wire,
Dreams of nuts that never tire.
We wave to stars, they twinkle bright,
Winking back just out of sight.

In crowded rooms, ideas fly,
Like paper airplanes way too high.
We chase them down with cups of tea,
While pondering what 'should be' could be.

Yet as we tumble through this maze,
Laughter fills our aimless phase.
In every jest, a nugget dwells,
A cosmic joke that fate compels.

Lost in a Maze of Wonder

A hedgehog spins an endless tale,
Of life's grand journey on a snail.
It wears a crown of dandelion fluff,
Claiming wisdom is just too tough.

In circles we run, like children at play,
Chasing thoughts that swirl away.
'Why are we here?' a duckling quacks,
The answer lies in having snacks!

Fish in the pond give disapproving looks,
As we debate like silly books.
Each ripple giggles, waves a fin,
Life's big mystery: where to begin?

While traversing paths, we laugh and cheer,
For joy's the answer that feels most clear.
In this funny dance, we find our way,
With every chuckle, we're here to stay.

The Unraveling of Everything

Once I sought the great 'what's next,'
But ended up at spoons and texts.
A rabbit in a waistcoat said,
'You're more confused, just eat some bread!'

We ride the waves of curious fate,
While socks debate their mismatched state.
A bouncy ball declares with flair,
'Life's a party if you just dare!'

In gardens where the butterflies toast,
To pinatas of wisdom, we laugh the most.
Each swing and miss, a lesson learned,
In the game of life, the prize is turned.

So come, let's spin in silly circles,
In this grand quest, let laughter twirl.
For as we unravel, stitch by stitch,
We find joy in being a little rich.

Shadows of Inquiry

In shadows deep, we search and tread,
With thoughts that bounce inside our head.
Questions fly like birds in the sky,
While answers hide and giggle by.

We ponder life with a furrowed brow,
While snorting laughter may show us how.
Every riddle met with playful cheer,
Turns our frowns to giggles sincere.

Is it the cake, or the frosting sweet?
Or maybe the cat that's missing a beat?
In each fine mess of eccentricity,
Lies a riddle wrapped in hilarity.

So bring your queries, let's give a cheer,
For pondering's fun, with friends so dear.
In twilight's glow, we'll question away,
With laughter echoing, come what may.

The Infinite Question

Why do we laugh when skies turn gray?
Just to mask what we dare not say.
With each twist of fate, we giggle more,
At puzzles stacked like laundry on the floor.

Each moment's full of quirks and spins,
Like trying to jog in alligator skins.
Who's got the map to this quirky quest?
Let's spread our arms; we're truly blessed!

Like ducks in rows, we waddle about,
In search of wisdom wrapped in doubt.
With rubber ducks floating in our tea,
Who knew that life could be so zany?

Here's to us, all seekers of cheer!
We'll trip on thoughts that feel so near.
In every laugh, the truth may be,
Life's greatest jest, a comedy spree!

Tides of Contemplation

The waves of thoughts come crashing in,
As we build our castles made of sin.
With beach balls bouncing in salty air,
We dive for answers trapped in despair.

What's that shimmer on the ocean wide?
Is it wisdom dressed in a fish's stride?
Or merely lunch on a sunny plate,
Echoing laughter as we contemplate?

Oh, life's a shore with tides that shift,
A merry-go-round with a goofy lift.
Let's surf the waves of inquiry bold,
With flip-flops on and stories untold.

So let's splash around in this mirthful tide,
Where questions dance with the ocean's pride.
With every gulp of salty bliss,
We question fate, with a wink and a kiss!

Reflections on a Blank Canvas

A canvas wide, so blank and bare,
Where thoughts collide without a care.
With splashes bright and colors loud,
We'll paint our dreams and make them proud.

What's that smudge with a hint of blue?
It could be madness or coffee too.
In strokes of joy, we picture the scene,
As laughter seals the in-between.

Each daub a quest, a quirky line,
Like scribbles from a toddler divine.
We'll spin and twirl with glee alight,
In searching hues of day and night.

So grab your brushes, let artwork flow,
In this funny dance of the unknown.
Each stroke a giggle, each line a chuckle,
As we paint our lives in whimsical shuffle.

Canvas of Unanswered Prayers

On a canvas of hopes, painted in gray,
The brush slips and flicks, bright colors sway.
I asked the universe, where's my sweet cake?
It chuckled and said, 'Your wish is a fake.'

All these scribbles, they dance in my mind,
Like socks in the dryer, just hard to find.
A masterpiece lost, in the mess so absurd,
Can laughter be art? Little joy is stirred.

Whispers from the Ether

In the corner, a whisper, so soft and unclear,
It tickles my thoughts, brings chuckles and cheer.
Is that wisdom I hear, or just the fridge hum?
Maybe both, but still, I feel kind of dumb.

A voice from the clouds, or just static in air,
I've asked for a sign, but it plays hard to share.
I ponder each riddle, while sipping my tea,
Maybe it's just my cat, judging me free.

Quicksand of Ambiguity

Stuck in this quicksand, confusion ensues,
Try to step forward, but I'm bound by my shoes.
Do I leap for the stars, or dig for some gold?
A map full of blur, is just getting old.

I laugh at my plight, while sinking right down,
The more that I struggle, the more I'll just drown.
Is the meaning a joke, a pun on my plight?
I'd rather it's funny, than just black and white.

The Maze of Introspection

Welcome to my maze, where thoughts twist and curl,
I took a wrong turn, and now I just twirl.
Should I follow my gut, or map out the route?
It feels like a circus; where's my prized lout?

Each corner I turn, mirrors laugh back at me,
'What's wrong, little mind? Come dance, be free!'
So I skip through the halls, with a grin on my face,
Maybe lost is the best, in this whimsical place.

Charting the Unknown

I set sail on seas so wide,
With a map made of spaghetti tied.
I seek answers to life's grand quest,
But all I find is my lunch to digest.

With each wave a ponderous thought,
Is that wisdom or just a joke I forgot?
A compass spins in a dizzy dance,
Leading me in circles, not even a chance.

What if the treasure I seek's a mirage?
A goldfish in a bowl, wearing a barrage.
I laugh at the skies, not sure what's wise,
Perhaps it's better to just eat fries.

So here I drift, with laughter my guide,
In a rowboat of hopes, with a dog by my side.
Each wave, a chuckle, a riddle or jest,
Maybe here, I'll simply find rest.

The Library of Inquiries

In a library stacked with dusty tomes,
I searched for truths, but found only gnomes.
Each query whispered, 'Do I exist?'
As I pulled a book, it turned into mist.

The librarian looked, a wink in his eye,
'You won't find answers, just questions that fly.'
I grabbed a chair, feeling quite clever,
To decipher the riddle, or at least, a lever.

A tome said, 'Why did the chicken cross?'
To find a good fable or just count the gloss?
As I chuckled and read, the hours slipped by,
Maybe life's a story, with reason awry.

So I'll shelf my musings, not fret or stew,
For each laugh is a clue, and folly too.
Between the pages, I find my own spark,
In the chaos of nonsense, I make my own mark.

Surrounded by the Unanswered

In a room stuffed with questions, I sit so alone,
Lost in a jungle of thoughts overthrown.
'Where's the exit?' I muse, as I scratch my head,
Surrounded by puzzles that just spread and spread.

The couch seems to chuckle while I take a seat,
It whispers, 'Relax, put your worries on repeat.'
Each riddle a puzzle I can't quite unfold,
Like socks from the dryer, they never come told.

Is it better to chase or to simply retreat?
A dance with the shadows of questions that greet.
While pondering all that I cannot discern,
I sip absurdity; it's my lesson to learn.

So let's toss our inquiries into the breeze,
They'll float around like dandelion seeds.
For among all the chaos, a grin shall prevail,
Being lost in the questions is where dreams set sail.

Light and Shadow of Thought

In the spotlight of reason, I stand with a grin,
Dancing with doubts, waltzing with sin.
'What is the truth?' I boldly proclaim,
While wearing mismatched socks, just for the game.

Shadows of wisdom flit past my face,
In a jig of absurdity, I find my own space.
Thoughts like confetti, they scatter and fall,
I chase after giggles, oblivious to all.

In the flicker of candlelight, ideas collide,
A burst of bright colors in the dark I confide.
Maybe the fun's in the questions we hold,
In the jests of our musings, true gems unfold.

So here's to the humor that burrows so deep,
To the quirks of existence that never lose sleep.
In the light and the shadows, I'll dance through the fray,
For every odd query makes for a fine play.

Echoes in the Silence

In the quiet, thoughts bounce around,
Question marks dance without a sound.
What's the puzzle? Who really knows?
Lost in laughter, as the confusion grows.

Philosophers sip tea, pondering deep,
While my socks vanish into a sleep.
Do ducks know why they quack and quirk?
Or is it just a daily perk?

With every riddle life throws my way,
I scribble notes but still mislay.
As giggles echo in the void's embrace,
I contemplate in this funny place.

So bring on the mystery, cheers to the quest!
For laughter and joy are simply the best.
Amidst the chaos, a chuckle will find,
Answers are funny, if you're open of mind.

Sunlight on a Gloomy Path

Wandering down a path so gray,
Searching for sunshine, come what may.
Footsteps shuffle, a dance in the mist,
Hoping for warmth, I clench my fist.

Why do clouds frown and block the sun?
Is there a reason for all this fun?
A thought jumps out like a jack-in-the-box,
Can we find joy in our quirky flocks?

Suddenly a grin breaks through the haze,
Tickling my ribs in bright, sunny ways.
Laughter's aroma fills the air,
As pine trees sway without a care.

Yet here I stand, in a light-hearted stride,
Finding bright moments with each silly ride.
Gloom may surround, but my spirit stays,
In jokes and quips, life's mood always sways.

Navigating the Unknown

Oh, the roads we travel, a twist and a turn,
With maps drawn in crayon, surely I'll learn.
Where's the compass? I've lost my way,
But chuckles abound in this grand display.

A sign says "Detour!" I laugh and I scoff,
While GPS says, "Make a U-turn, cough."
Exploring odd alleys, delightfully lost,
In pursuit of wisdom, I'm counting the cost.

With every misstep, a story is spun,
From penguin dances to a cow that can run.
As the universe giggles, I stumble and weave,
Finding treasures in laughter, oh how I believe!

So here's to the chaos, and all of the trails,
For life's a grand journey where humor prevails.
Let maps be ignored, with joy in my feast,
Navigating unknowns, I'm surely no beast.

Chasing Fleeting Revelations

Like butterflies flitting in a bright blue sky,
I chase fleeting moments that whisper and sigh.
With each little insight, I laugh with delight,
Only to lose them, like stars in the night.

"Eureka!" I shout, as ideas come fast,
But like a balloon, they pop and are past.
What was that gem? Ah, where did it flee?
I guess I'll just chase it, with maybe some glee.

Friends gather 'round in a fit of good cheer,
Trading our ponderings, holding them dear.
In silly debates about jelly or jam,
The world's full of wonders — oh yes, yes it can!

So I'll keep on laughing as thoughts swirl and dance,
For life's little questions deserve more than a glance.
Let's revel in whimsy, with joy as our guide,
Chasing those moments — what futures beside?

Flickering Lights of Understanding

In a world of tangled wires,
We search for flickers bright.
Questions dance like fireflies,
But clarity's out of sight.

We twist and turn through darkened halls,
With laughter in our stride.
Chasing shadows on the walls,
And giggling at our pride.

The lightbulb fizzles, pops, and hums,
Each flicker brings a grin.
We journey through confusion's drums,
And let the chaos spin.

So let's embrace this funny game,
As we juggle all our thoughts.
In this circus of the strange,
The wisdom we have sought.

Beyond the Veil of Perception

Peeking through reality's veil,
We ponder what's concealed.
With a wink and knowing smile,
Our thoughts prepare to yield.

The universe rolls its eyes at fate,
As we fumble through each day.
We juggle facts, relate, then wait,
For meaning in dismay.

Cosmic jokes float in the air,
As meaning hides and plays.
Yet in this chaos, we declare,
We'll dance through all the haze.

So wave to stars that twinkle bright,
And don't forget to laugh.
For in this dizzying cosmic fight,
We'll find our silly path.

Conversations with the Universe

Chatting up the moon and stars,
We share our doubts and fears.
The cosmos giggles at our scars,
And gently wipes our tears.

We argue with the sun at dawn,
Who laughs at all our schemes.
In silence, every night we've drawn,
We're tangled in our dreams.

Questions tumble from our lips,
Like popcorn in the air.
The Milky Way just does some flips,
While we pretend to care.

So let's keep these talks alive,
With laughter in the mix.
For every thought we seek to thrive,
The universe plays tricks.

Charting the Uncharted

With maps of clouds and stars in hand,
We set our course for fun.
Through lands where no one dares to stand,
We giggle, one by one.

Our compass spins, it doesn't care,
As we wander far and wide.
Each misstep leads us somewhere rare,
With joy we can't abide.

In uncharted thoughts, we trip and fall,
But laughter lights the way.
We'll sketch our dreams upon the wall,
And paint them bright as day.

So here's to paths that twist and turn,
With each wrong path we find.
For in this playful way we learn,
The treasure's in the mind.

Footprints in the Sand of Time

On the beach, I lost my way,
Chasing seagulls that would sway.
Footprints belong to those who roam,
But mine lead straight back to my home.

Waves crash loud, the tide rolls in,
I ponder where my thoughts have been.
A sandcastle built to impress,
Collapsed by waves, I must confess.

Seashells whisper secrets untold,
But even they can't make me bold.
What's the point of all this sand?
Do we really understand?

Laughter echoes, as I slip,
In the ocean, do I dip?
Life's a joke with a punchline late,
Let's just dance, it's never too late.

Searching for Clarity in the Mist

Walking through fog that's thick and gray,
I tripped on thoughts that seemed to stray.
Searching hard for some clear view,
But the mist says, "Not today, boo!"

Ghostly shadows flicker near,
Are they friends, or is it fear?
I'll ask a tree, I might get wise,
But it just rustles, no replies.

Out here, logic makes no sense,
Every step feels like pretense.
What's that I hear, a distant chime?
Could it be clearer thoughts? Or just slime?

Yet in this haze, I must admit,
There's humor found in every bit.
Laughing at how lost I've strayed,
The trees just giggle, I'm unafraid.

Unfolding the Unknowable

Life's a puzzle, pieces askew,
I've lost the box, I can't construe.
Each step I take, a twist and turn,
What's the lesson? When will I learn?

Unfolding mysteries, like a map,
I can't quite grasp, it's all a flap.
Instructions read like ancient Greek,
I sigh and smile, stay quirky, unique.

A fortune cookie once did say,
"True wisdom hides in playful play."
So here I sit, confused and dazed,
Yet finding joy in the crazed.

So let's embrace the mystery,
Perhaps it's just a history.
With laughter as my guiding light,
I'll dance through life, take flight tonight!

In Pursuit of Tomorrow's Truth

Dashing forward, running fast,
Chasing truths that seldom last.
Tomorrow whispers in my ear,
But today's antics bring good cheer.

Glimpses of what's just ahead,
Maybe it's cake, or freshly bred.
But what's the point, I question now,
When today's jokes make me go wow?

Lighthearted steps on this weird quest,
Each riddle's just a funny jest.
Do I need answers, or just to play?
Why not just laugh through the day?

So here I stand, a silly fool,
In search of wisdom? Not in school!
Perhaps the truth's a wobbly dance,
Join me now, take a chance!

Beneath the Surface of Consciousness

In a world of deep questions, we float,
Like ducks on a pond, we stay remote.
Thoughts bubble up, but then they dive,
We giggle and wonder, do we really thrive?

On a quest for truth, we sip our tea,
Discussing the meaning of a goldfish's glee.
Philosophers ponder, but they can't decide,
If a cat really knows it's a cat that hides!

In dreams we chase answers in a race,
But land on our faces in a comical place.
With socks on our hands, we dance through the gloom,
Consciousness, oh consciousness, you've lost your room!

So here we sit, in our silly attire,
Asking ourselves if we should retire.
With laughter we ponder life's curious schemes,
In this wacky realm of our wildest dreams!

Dancing on the Edge of Doubt

On the edge of the unknown, we prance and sway,
With one shoe on, we make our own way.
Is that a thought or simply a breeze?
We giggle and twirl, hoping to tease.

Jumping around like a bouncy ball,
Doubt is just laughter wearing a shawl.
We ask the big questions, with a wink and a nod,
If cheese is alive, does it feel like a god?

Waltzing with whimsy, we trip and we spin,
Falling on answers that never begin.
In this dance, we find joy in the mess,
Because floating in doubt, we're truly blessed!

So let's raise a toast with our cups full of tea,
To odd little thoughts that set our minds free.
For in this grand cha-cha of cosmic jest,
We're all just the same—chasing life's quest!

The Weight of Unasked Questions

Unasked questions hang in the air,
Like socks left behind in a strange pair.
They float like balloons that refuse to pop,
While we giggle and ask, 'Will they ever stop?'

With heavy thoughts, we walk like drunks,
Stumbling on answers like a pile of punk.
Could a fish wear a hat, or is that too much?
We laugh at the nonsense, oh such a touch!

While pondering life on this whimsical ride,
We glance at the clouds as they gently slide.
Skipping through doubts with shoes made of foam,
Unasked questions feel just like home!

So let's cradle our queries with a chuckle and cheer,
As we float through the chaos, swigging down beer.
For in the weight of questions that never arose,
We find silly answers, that's just how it goes!

A Tapestry of Uncertainty

In the fabric of thoughts, we weave and jive,
Colors of doubt keep us alive.
With stitches of laughter and threads of glee,
We quilt our confusion like bees on a spree.

Tangled in riddles, we poke and prod,
Is why just a cover for a grumpy old cod?
Questions in patterns that never quite form,
Creating a chaos where silliness warms.

With each little knot that we craft and create,
We toss in a pun, isn't that great?
For even in chaos, there's joy to be found,
In the tapestry woven, spinning round and round.

So grab your old yarn and let's knit up a tale,
Of mysteries hidden in laughter's own veil.
For in uncertainty, there's a dance we can share,
Creating bright tapestries for all to declare!

Searching for the Morning Star

In the sky so wide and bright,
I seek that twinkling light.
Is it lost? Or just asleep?
Maybe it's planning a leap.

Coffee spills upon my shirt,
My search, it seems, is for dessert.
Stars can wait, I'll take a bite,
Of cake that calls me every night.

Should I write my own dear star?
Or ask the moon if it's too far?
Whispers of fate in skies so vast,
Like my Netflix queue, it grows fast.

So here's to bright celestial trips,
With cupcakes and donut flips.
The morning star might play coy,
Yet pastry treats bring me joy!

The Weight of What Lies Unsaid

I ponder deep on awkward cues,
Like heavy shoes in a game of twos.
Words piled high on a teetering stack,
What could I say? I might lose track.

My dog's wise eyes hold all my thoughts,
He listens close, but he's not got pots.
Should I speak, or should I bark,
In this funny, silent park?

Meanwhile, the cats just plot and scheme,
While I consider my next dream.
What holds more weight—a sigh or laugh?
Is there a scale? Let's do the math!

Unsaid things float like jellybeans,
Giggling softly, a candy theme.
So I'll let thoughts bounce and drift,
Laughter's my only gift!

A Parable of Shadows and Light

Shadows dance in the midday sun,
They flip and flop, oh what fun!
But why do they never say a word?
Are they misunderstood, or just perturbed?

Light beams smile with radiant cheer,
While shadows whisper, 'It's too clear!'
They plot and play, this twisted game,
While I just seek to find my fame.

Do shadows long for the golden glow?
Or do they just want help to grow?
I ask the sun, it shrugs and beams,
'Both shadows and light have silly dreams!'

A parable ignites in this dusky space,
Where laughter hides behind each face.
Let's embrace the quirks, join the show,
For every shadow, there's light to throw!

The Intimacy of Undecided

I stood at the fridge, heart in a spin,
Should I snack on leftovers? Where to begin?
Carrots or cake? A brave life choice,
But I just keep hearing my inner voice.

Decisions, decisions, come play with me!
Like squirrels on branches, so wild and free.
In this existential culinary plight,
Is ice cream a dream or a savory bite?

So I flip a coin, heads means treat,
Tails just means shuffle my feet.
This intimacy sparks as time ticks on,
Embarking on snacks till the break of dawn.

In the end, I hear my tummy's cheer,
As the fridge door swings wide, with no fear.
Life's a buffet, so let's make a bet,
And laugh at decisions we won't regret!

Reflections in the Abyss

In a deep, dark well, I ponder
Why do ducks quack and not wander?
I scratch my head, while sipping tea,
Is it all just cosmic irony?

Stars twinkle above, all so bright,
While I trip over shoes in the night.
Is that a comet or just my cat?
Life's riddles wrapped in a strange hat.

The universe hums a baffling tune,
With socks that vanish each afternoon.
I chase a thought, it slips away,
Maybe laughter is here to stay.

So here I sit, pondering more,
Is it pizza or the universe at the core?
With a wink and a nudge, I float along,
In this galactic dance, I'll sing my song.

Wanderer in the Void

I float through the void, oh so free,
In search of a snack, or just some peace.
Cosmic dust tastes like stale bread,
And I wonder what's wrong with my head.

A dance of the stars, a flicker of light,
But I'm tripping over meteors tonight.
Galaxies spin, but I just yawn,
Is it midnight or just the crack of dawn?

A jellyfish floats by, gives me a wave,
It says, "Chill out, you don't need to behave!"
I smile back, in this endless space,
With giggles echoing, I find my place.

So I drift on with cosmic flair,
Forget the pressure, just breathe the air.
The snacks may be few, the laughs are grand,
Life's a mystery, let whimsy stand.

The Enigma of Existence

Why do we smile and then we sigh?
Are we all just stars in a cosmic pie?
Like cats that plot with conspiracies,
    Life's a circus of oddities.

Fairies dance on the tips of my toes,
While pondering why the garden grows.
    Is it magic or just plain luck,
That leads me through this space of muck?

Fish swim by in this curious dream,
Do they wonder about the moonbeam?
    I toss a coin, watch it spin,
    As I try to decide if it's a win.

So I laugh with my existential dread,
Counting all the times I've misread.
The world spins on, with joy or strife,
It's just one big, strange slice of life.

Fragments of a Fading Illumination

A light bulb flickers, then it goes dim,
As I contemplate the cosmic whim.
Are socks left behind in a parallel land?
Or just a plot woven by a hand?

The toaster pops, sings its sweet song,
As I question where do I belong.
With crumbs of thoughts strewn all about,
I giggle and dance, banishing doubt.

Do aliens know when tea is brewed?
And why does my cat look extremely shrewd?
I ponder these questions, one slice at a time,
As I laugh with the universe, fading in rhyme.

So let the stars twinkle in their outfits grand,
Life's a cosmic joke not fully planned.
With fragments of light and humor made,
I'll laugh on through the cosmic parade.

Whispers in the Void

In the cosmos, I lost my sock,
Floating with stars, what a shock!
Planets are laughing, I'm confused,
Should I be enlightened or just amused?

Comets speeding, they give me a wink,
While black holes drown me, I start to think.
Is it all a joke or a cosmic prank?
I'll toast to the void, let's fill up my tank!

Unwritten Chapters of Existence

Life's a book, but I lost my pen,
Pages still turn, where've I been?
A plot twist here, and a sketch right there,
Just trying to figure out what I should wear.

The chapters jump, like a cat on a kite,
Fleeting ideas, keep me up at night.
With coffee in hand, I scribble away,
Hoping to stumble on a bright sunny day.

Echoes of an Unfinished Quest

I set out on a quest with a map upside down,
Searching for answers in a bustling town.
The guide just chuckled, then pointed to fries,
"You'll find the wisdom in greasy surprise!"

Backpack full of snacks, compass in tow,
I asked the wise owl, he didn't know.
With a wink and a hoot, he flew off to eat,
Guess I'll just follow my own two left feet!

Questions Between Stars

Starlight whispers of secrets untold,
But they giggle and dance, too bold!
"Do we have purpose?" I ask the night sky,
The stars just twinkle, "Why even try?"

Galaxies collide with a hiccup or two,
Creating a mess, like a cosmic stew.
Between the stars, I'd like to know,
If life's a show, where's my front row?

A Journey Yet Undiscovered

With GPS broken, we wander wide,
Maps are obsolete, but we stride.
Each step a question, without a clue,
Where's the destination? Oh, who knew?

We laugh at signs pointing nowhere fast,
Collecting moments, making them last.
Is it the journey or the snacks we find?
Maybe the answer's in the chocolate kind?

In fields of daisies, we give a sigh,
Dreaming of answers that float on by.
Do we need answers, or is this just fun?
Let's dance in the chaos, worry undone!

So here's to roads that twist and turn,
For every misstep, there's still much to learn.
Life's a weird riddle, no need to race,
With a chuckle, we embrace the chase!

The Dialogues of Uncertainty

Two squirrels argue up in a tree,
Is life a joke or a grand mystery?
One says 'Chase nuts, that's all it takes!'
The other just giggles, for goodness' sakes!

What if they're wrong? They munch and ponder,
While pondering makes their tails grow fonder.
In the absurdity of existence they find,
A secret to live, with a dash of unwind!

"Then why the rain?" asks the one with glee,
"Are we just puddles, or do we flee?"
They debate the cosmos, with hearts so light,
Sprinkling nonsense in the fading light.

Their conversation drifts as day turns to night,
With giggles and nonsense, it feels just right.
In the chaos of thoughts, they find a sweet bliss,
For life's silly questions, they share a sweet kiss!

Musings Beneath the Surface

In the bathtub, thoughts float away,
Why does soap suds dance and sway?
Rubber ducks join with curious glee,
Philosophers lost in a sea of tea!

Bubble baths hold the weight of the world,
While imaginations are tossed and twirled.
Each splash a riddle, a whimsy tale,
Is this the meaning, or just a whale?

Shampoo bottles preach the good life trend,
But is that luxury just make pretend?
We scrub our doubts down the drain with a laugh,
Maybe insights come in the post-bath aftermath!

As the water cools and the daylight fades,
We giggle at thoughts, unafraid parades.
In the warmth of foam, we discover the truth,
Life's greatest joy is simply aloof!

Ripples of Thought in the Abyss

In the depths of a pond, ideas collide,
Frog philosophers croak with pride.
Each ripple whispers secrets so deep,
Contemplating mysteries, their promises to keep.

A fish jumps up, seeking a veil,
"Why swim in circles? Is that the trail?"
The turtles reply with a sage-like nod,
"It's not just the end, it's the path, oh my God!"

The dragonflies hover, making it clear,
Life's a quick dance without a clear steer.
With wings of laughter, they zoom through the air,
Finding meaning in moments, free from all care.

So wander we will, with our giddy hearts,
Unraveling life's canvas with quirky arts.
In the ripples below, and the giggles above,
We find our own answers, wrapped up in love!

Roads Untraveled and Paths Untold

I took a leap, my map a mess,
With twists and turns, I must confess.
A goat stood still, as if to say,
"Do you even know? Or lost your way?"

Each step I take, new signs arise,
Like ducks in hats, oh what a sight!
They quack their thoughts, so wise, yet bold,
"Just follow us, we've got the gold!"

The trees all chuckle, branches sway,
As I ponder what they'll say today.
I ask a squirrel, with twitching tail,
"Is your nut stash worth this wild tale?"

In alleys broad and corners tight,
I dance with shadows, in the night.
"Where does this lead?" I scratch my head,
"It's a surprise," the universe said.

Navigating the Depths of Curiosity.

A fish in pants, swam through the door,
"Excuse me, sir, but what's the score?"
With googly eyes and fins so bright,
He held a map to bizarre delight.

"Let's dive right in!" he splashed around,
"Exploration's grand, let's break new ground!"
The jellybeans float, in colors so neat,
And every sweet brings laughter, a treat!

With curious tones, we plotted our quest,
To find the place that's fond of jest.
"Is this really real?" I gasped and grinned,
He winked back, "In dreams, my friend!"

Reality bends, a rubbery stretch,
While giggling stars start to fetch.
"I'll ask the sun!" my fish friend declares,
"Hold on tight; we'll outsmart our cares!"

Existential Whispers

In the quiet night, where thoughts do tease,
Philosophers chat, with cups of cheese.
"Why are we here?" one loudly wondered,
The moon shrugged back, all bright and thundered.

Birds in bow ties took flight with flair,
"Life's just a game, so fill the air!"
They flipped and flapped, with splendid grace,
Inviting clouds to join the race.

Meanwhile, a cactus wearing a frown,
Spoke of love in a prickly town.
"Don't overthink, my needle-point friend,
Sometimes it's okay to just pretend!"

Swaying shadows danced in glee,
Echoing giggles—such sweet decree.
"What is the point?" they chimed along,
"There's joy in chaos, come sing our song!"

Searching for Stars

Beneath the sky, so vast, so wide,
I climbed a tree for a cosmic ride.
With jelly-filled dreams, I reached up high,
"Is there a map to the stars?" I cry.

A raccoon grinned, with eyes aglow,
"Just grab a snack and let's not go slow!"
He munches on cookies, crumbs in flight,
As fireflies twinkle, a wondrous sight.

We slipped on clouds, which squeaked and squealed,
Tickling toes, oh, what a field!
"With every giggle, a star is born,
The universe laughs at the tales we scorn!"

The moon, now chuckling, joined our spree,
"Just keep on dreaming, be just like me."
Through cosmic chuckles, we danced so far,
Searching aloud for the next shooting star!

An Inquiry at Twilight

As the sun dips low, I ponder and squint,
Why did the chicken cross, did it leave a hint?
Questions bounce around like a wayward kite,
   Searching for sense in the fading twilight.

My goldfish nods, he's a wise little guy,
"Just swim in circles, don't question the sky."
I ask him more, he gives me a stare,
Maybe he knows, or he simply don't care.

A cat leaps atop my puzzled old chair,
"Life's just a game, are you willing to share?"
I scratch my head as the dog rolls his eyes,
So many questions, yet nobody's wise.

At twilight's end, I grab my old book,
Searching for answers, or maybe a look,
But all I find is the same silly tune,
"Just laugh it all off, you'll get it by noon!"

The Fabric of Inquiry

In the loom of my mind, I weave threads so tight,
Spinning old queries in the soft morning light.
What's life? A riddle dressed up in a rhyme,
Or a sock with a hole that we've worn out of time?

My coffee cup laughs as I sip and I stare,
"Do spoonfuls of sugar equal wisdom?" I dare.
A spoon drops its wisdom, it clinks on my mug,
Filled with sweet questions, the fuzziness snug.

I toss out my net in this sea of a thought,
Catching some giggles that life's tightly wrought.
"Catch me a fish with a sense of the real!"
Said one tiny fish, with a wink and a squeal.

I thread through existence with fabric unspooled,
Seeking the lesson life carefully schooled.
Yet here I am, stitching patches of fun,
While life plays charades, and I'm still on the run.

Waves of the Unseen

At the shore of my brain, the waves crash and roll,
Bringing bits of nonsense, like seaweed in a bowl.
What floats on the surface, what hides in the deep?
Questions like jellyfish, just drifting in sleep.

The tide pulls me in, with the charm of a jest,
"Dive in!" it whispers, "Just give it your best!"
But I hesitate, what if I can't swim?
The sea seems to giggle, it's not looking grim.

A seagull swoops low, "Hey, what's all the fuss?"
"Why ask about meaning? Just enjoy the bus!"
With feathers of wisdom, it flits out of sight,
Leaving behind echoes of laughter and light.

So here I will stand, on this beach made of thoughts,
Building sandcastles with all of my oughts.
And though waves may be wild, and none seem to know,
I'll ride the foam, and just go with the flow.

Threads of the Unspeakable

In the attic of dreams, I stumble and trip,
Over boxes of questions with no real grip.
Dust bunnies giggle, they're wise little folks,
Gathering stories, and weaving in jokes.

"What's the key to it all?" I gasp in despair,
But a laughing old shoe says, "Life's fair and square!"
My shoelace unties, it begins to unwind,
A tangled up mess, just as I often find.

A squirrel pops out, with a nut in his cheeks,
"Friend, why worry? Just play hide and seek!"
His wisdom shines bright, like a bright candy shell,
While I sit and ponder, still caught in my spell.

So I'll weave these new threads, of laughter and cheer,
As the squirrels hold court and the dust bunnies leer.
For in all of this chaos, we get lost in the fun,
And the world feels so light when we dance in the sun.

Bridges Over Gaps of Understanding

Thoughts like bridges sway and bend,
Some believe they're broken, my friend.
We laugh and joke, we scratch our heads,
Who knew pondering led to such dreads?

Cups half empty, cups half full,
Balance tips, it's mighty dull.
But in this silliness, we find the spark,
To navigate life's grand old park.

Wit can dance on shaky ground,
If you listen, you might be found.
Behind each flap and each misstep,
A chorus of chuckles, the best concept!

Clumsy paths and jumbled speech,
Are there secrets out of reach?
Maybe the truth's a funny bone,
That keeps us laughing, never alone.

Mirror of Uncertain Reflections

A mirror chats without a clue,
Reflecting thoughts, all mine and you.
It shows my socks, mismatched and odd,
Cackling with a silent nod.

Selfies taken with a grin,
Each angle hides the thoughts within.
In each fond smile, a question lies,
What's hiding underneath those eyes?

We ponder while we face the glass,
What's real? What's make-believe? What's sass?
But in this game of peeking deep,
We find it's laughter that we keep.

Models of what could be, should be,
Yet here we stand, all goofy, free.
Mirrors can flare, distort and bend,
Still, they're our buddies till the end.

Collisions of Thought and Time

Time's a jester with a wink,
Thoughts collide, then pause to think.
Do minutes laugh, or just roll by?
I'm here to ponder, oh my, oh my!

Tick-tock goes a clock as I guess,
Am I lost in thought or a tangled mess?
Like socks that vanish in my drawer,
We search for answers, but find no score.

Jamming thoughts on the highway of fate,
Each idea collides, it's quite the date.
Is it profound? Or just plain silly?
Life's a riddle, and it's never frilly.

Yet amidst each crash, a grin emerges,
For bumbles and fumbles build the urges.
So let's collide with our minds in play,
Tomorrow's mystery is here today!

A Map without Directions

Here's my map, but where to go?
X marks the spot, but I don't know.
With squiggly lines and colors bright,
I'm lost in laughter, what a sight!

"Turn left at chaos, then take a right,
Cross over giggles, and hang a slight.
Look for the cloud shaped like a sheep,
And there you'll find the truth you seek!"

But what if the sheep is busy munching?
Lost in thought, and endlessly crunching.
It's a wild ride, both here and there,
Directions? Who needs 'em? Just share a dare!

So here's to wandering with no great plan,
Maps that change with every fan.
We'll chase our laughs, not some dull goal,
Finding joy is the ultimate role.

When Certainty Remains Elusive

In search of truth, we roam the halls,
Chasing shadows, bouncing off walls.
With maps that lead to nowhere near,
We laugh aloud, the end is unclear.

A chicken crossed a road, we see,
Is it lost, or just wild and free?
Philosophers ponder in grand debate,
While we snack on chips and contemplate.

The puzzle pieces never align,
But pizza's here, so we'll be just fine.
In gaps of thought, our giggles ring,
While searching for wisdom, it's pizza we bring.

Perhaps the squirrels hold the key,
To secrets that we can't foresee.
With every nut they gather tight,
We wonder if they've got it right!

The Space Between Answers

In realms of questions, we twirl and spin,
Exploring the chaos, where to begin?
A riddle walks in wearing a grin,
It sips from a cup, as if to say 'win.'

What's orange but not a fruit, I ask?
The silence deepens, a difficult task.
The clock ticks loud, wisdom takes flight,
While we clutch our snacks, debating what's right.

At times, the answers wear silly hats,
Dance like penguins, or play with bats.
Between questions and laughs, the joy expands,
Stuck somewhere, yet holding life's hands.

With questions we'll wander, we'll laugh too loud,
In this silly quest, we're strangely proud.
For in the gaps, we'll find delight,
And giggle together into the night.

Dreams Linger in the Twilight

As day drifts off, and night takes the stage,
My dreams put on a curious page.
With unicorns flying and donuts that talk,
Each whimsy leads us on a whimsical walk.

"Is there a point?" the owls hoot low,
As fireflies wink, all aglow.
In the quiet moment, whispers of fate,
Chuckle and giggle in this twilight state.

An elephant juggles, a turtle will dance,
While riddles surround us in a curious trance.
The answers elude, but laughter does soar,
In dreams where reality opens the door.

So let's hold these moments with quirky delight,
As we chase the fuzzies through the soft night.
In wonderment, we play and convene,
With dreams twinkling on every screen.

Pathways of the Intrigued Mind

In the maze of thought, I found a door,
Through it spilled laughter, so much to explore.
With maps drawn in crayon, bright as can be,
We ventured forth, just my thoughts and me.

"Why does toast land butter-side down?"
I ponder in silence, wearing a frown.
But a smirk breaks through, as I trip on a shoe,
And thoughts of the universe start coming in two.

With questions like balloons, floating high,
Each answer's a launchpad into the sky.
A rollercoaster ride of whimsical finds,
In pathways, we stumble, we're curious minds!

So let's skip together down this odd lane,
Where questions are silly, and laughter the gain.
For in the pursuit of the wonderful ride,
We discover more joy when we glide side by side.

www.ingramcontent.com/pod-product-compliance
Lightning Source LLC
Chambersburg PA
CBHW051651160426
43209CB00004B/879